Nature's Fury

California Burning!

by Meish Goldish

Wild Winds

by Amy Jolin

GLOBE FEARON

Pearson Learning Group

Contents

California Burning!

Wild Winds

California Burning!

by Meish Goldish

Chapter 1

Fire, Fire Everywhere!

Imagine you are sleeping when suddenly the sharp smell of smoke wakens you. Outside your bedroom window you see a giant wall of flames rolling across your neighbors' yards. Fire! The fast-moving blaze will be at your doorstep any minute, so you must act immediately. What do you do?

That's a question that thousands of panicked residents of Southern California faced in the fall of 2003. During a 2-week period in October and November, the state experienced the worst wildfires it has ever seen. Eleven **perilous** blazes raged out of control, spreading from community to community, in five counties. More than 100,000 people had to abandon their homes.

By the time all the fires finally **subsided**, they had burned more than 800,000 acres, or about 1,250 square miles. That's **virtually** the size of the state of Rhode Island. About 3,000 homes went up in smoke, and 20 people died. One California sheriff called it "the greatest fire tragedy in the history of this country."

Why Were These Fires So Bad?

In one sense, the Southern California wildfires of 2003 were not surprising. After all, wildfires have occurred in the forests, mountains, and canyons there for thousands of years. The fires come annually, usually in the summer and fall, when temperatures are high and the air is dry. They may **originate** from a bolt of lightning or a carelessly tossed match. The blazes spread quickly, **induced** by high, hot winds that push the flames forward.

Yet the wildfires of 2003 were **significantly** worse than any previous blazes in the recorded history of the state. In the past, wildfires destroyed trees and other vegetation but did little harm to individuals or homes.

Firefighters in Southern California battled wildfires like this one in the fall of 2003.

Until recently, few people lived in the mountains and canyons of Southern California. In recent years, however, all that has changed. Tens of thousands of Southern Californians have sought out the rugged wild land as a peaceful place to live. They have built homes on tree-lined hills and in steep canyons and valleys. Relaxing on their porches, they can enjoy breathtaking views of the forests, lakes, and cliffs that surround them.

Southern Californians have settled in the wild lands—but at a price. Now, if there's a fire in the area, they're a part of it. Rescues are not easy, either, because just a single winding road often leads to and from a mountain home or canyon ranch.

Even so, the California wildfires of 2003 shocked the nation. Americans wondered how such a tragedy could have occurred today. They wondered how the fires got so out of control and did such **extensive** damage. After all, our country has highly trained firefighters and first-rate equipment to battle blazes. So why weren't these wildfires put out sooner?

The answer is fascinating but not simple. It involves many factors, including when, where, and how the wildfires **originated** and spread. To gain a full understanding of the situation, it is best to start at the beginning of this amazing but true story.

Chapter 2

The Blazes Begin

Around midnight on Saturday, October 25, 2003, a hunter got lost in the wooded mountains near Ramona, California. He lit a small signal fire to draw the attention of his hunting partner in the area. Unfortunately, he didn't realize that his fire would easily spread. The hungry flames **vigorously** burned the dry brush—small trees, plants, and bushes—around him. The hunter escaped unhurt, but his fire was soon out of control.

It wasn't the only wildfire that began in Southern California that day. About 80 miles away, in San Bernardino county, witnesses saw two men throw something in the brush to start a fire. Unlike the hunter, however, these men were not in need of help. They were arsonists, people who set fires simply to destroy property. The arsonists' fire, like the one near Ramona, spread rapidly.

Earlier that same week, four other large wildfires had broken out in Southern California. By Monday, October 27, five more fires had begun. In all, 11 major wildfires were now burning **vigorously** in five different counties. Some were set by arsonists. Some fires began by accident. All were spreading rapidly.

Conditions for Disaster

The wildfires spread quickly for several reasons. First, the trees in the wild lands were very close to one another. When flames reached a treetop, they easily jumped to other treetops nearby. These jumping flames created a "crown fire" that quickly burned the upper level of trees in the area.

Also, bark beetles had recently attacked many of the trees in Southern California. These harmful insects suck the water out of wood, leaving a tree dry and weak, if not dead. Such a tree burns much faster than a healthy tree. The brush, too, was very dry, due to a serious lack of rain. Some parts of Southern California hadn't received rain in 4 years.

Finally, the fires traveled rapidly because of the Santa Ana winds. They are hot, dry desert winds that blow through Southern California in the fall. They blow at speeds up to 70 miles an hour. Once the wildfires began, the winds quickly spread the flames. The deadly fires, moving among crowded trees, dead wood, and dry vegetation made thousands of Southern Californians run for their lives.

The California wildfires stretched from north of Los Angeles all the way to the border of Mexico.

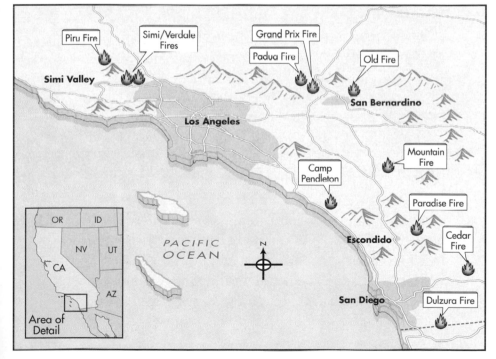

Frantic Escapes

"It was like the end of the world was going on. It was dark and flames were coming over the top, and we ran for it and we didn't think—with what we were running from—that there would be anything at all left, least of all our house." That's how one person described the scene as he desperately fled his home in Scripps Ranch, a canyon community in San Diego County. He was **striving** to escape the Cedar Fire—the one that had been set accidentally by a hunter near Ramona.

The Cedar Fire was the largest of the 11 fires now ablaze in Southern California. It was traveling especially fast. When Scripps Ranch residents woke to find flames licking at the trees on their property, they had no **alternative** but to leave their homes immediately. There was no time even to save any personal belongings. People jumped into their cars. They blew their horns to alert neighbors as they hurriedly drove away. Some used cell phones to warn family and friends in the area of the oncoming blazes.

In communities all over Southern California, similar scenes were occurring. With the rapid approach of each new wildfire, thousands of residents had to abandon their homes. Many received no warning at all of the oncoming flames being driven by the fierce Santa Ana winds.

In one case, a phone call that was made by mistake helped save many lives. One homeowner woke in the middle of the night and smelled smoke. Still half-asleep, she meant to call her cousin to warn her. Instead she accidentally dialed her sister. Her sister's husband then phoned other neighbors. Soon the entire neighborhood was empty.

Sadly, not everyone succeeded in escaping. In San Bernardino county, a 70-year-old man had a fatal heart attack while running from his home. A 93-year-old man died while watching his house go up in flames. Two teenagers were killed in a fire when flames forced their car off the road.

The fast-moving wildfires raced through neighborhoods and stunned thousands of Southern Californians.

Car escapes were especially **perilous** in canyon communities. Roads there are often narrow and twisting. Many are bumpy and unpaved as well. To worsen matters, some roads have no lights to help drivers see in the dark. Despite these difficulties, people made heroic attempts to get away. One man raced in his truck with his family. Then trouble **intervened**. When flames blocked the road, the family quickly abandoned the vehicle and ran to a riverbed. Fortunately, that split-second decision saved their lives.

In a similar dramatic situation, a husband and wife escaped flames that raced toward their home by jumping into their swimming pool. From the water, they could see their windows exploding as the fire burned their house to the ground. They felt grateful to be alive.

Officials said later that some lives were lost because people didn't follow orders. Some made the mistake of returning to their homes after evacuating. One woman went back to her ranch to save her horses. Sadly, the blazes trapped her before she could escape.

"The most important thing is your life and the lives of your children and family," emphasized a San Diego County official. Few people would **dispute** that statement. Yet many residents were confused because it wasn't clear whether or not they needed to evacuate. In some communities, fire officials first told residents to leave their homes. Then, the Santa Ana winds shifted, and officials said that people could return home. Hours later, however, the winds changed again, and the fires blew back in their direction. Once again, people had to pack what they could and abandon their property.

One frustrated resident said, "This is so nerve-racking. One minute you think you're okay, then all of a sudden it's coming toward you."

Even with **justifiable** warnings, many residents found it difficult to leave their homes immediately. Some stopped to gaze in disbelief at the distant blazes. Despite the oncoming **peril**, people were reluctant to leave their property. As one resident put it, "It's my house. I live here."

Sharon Robinson sat in her car with her daughter. They briefly watched the flames on the horizon before driving away. "We've lived in our home for 35 years," Robinson later recalled. "Fire has always stopped in the foothills. I never thought it would reach our home."

When time allowed, residents saved what little they could before leaving their homes. Dave Klueck was one of the lucky ones. Before he and his family drove off, they were able to pack some of their belongings in the car. They grabbed a change of clothing, some tools, family photographs, and home movies.

"There was a little bit of time to think about these things. But as soon as you stop, you're thinking of other things you would like to pitch in," Klueck sighed. "But you have only so much time, so you do what you can."

Some residents **strived** to protect their homes as best they could before having to abandon them. While the wildfires still raged in the distance, they frantically used chain saws to cut down trees standing in their yards. They hoped to deprive the fire of the fuel it would need to reach their homes. Racing against time, they dragged tree logs, branches, and leaves away from the area. They also hosed down their houses in hopes of preventing them from burning.

The odds were against the residents, however. Despite their efforts, the force of the fires was too powerful. As one **skeptical** resident later put it, "It was too little too late."

Chapter 3

Tackling the Crisis

Try to imagine 11 hungry wildfires roaring out of control at once. Now try to imagine all 11 fires burning in the same general region. That's what was happening in Southern California on Monday, October 27, 2003. If you were an astronaut orbiting high above Earth that day, you would have seen the smoke and flames.

To people on the ground, the fires seemed to be everywhere. Some were giant walls of flames that raced along roads and highways. Other blazes burned **extensively** in mountains and forests. Still others were fiery lines that moved downward into steep valleys and canyons.

Firefighters faced the overwhelming task of trying to contain and control the **perilous** fires. A fire is said to be fully contained when it is completely surrounded by firefighters. A fire is fully controlled when the blazes are finally extinguished, or put out.

Thousands of firefighters fought the raging blazes across Southern California. At first, despite their best efforts, they waged a losing battle. By Monday, most of the fires were less than 20 percent contained. The rest of the fires hadn't **subsided** at all.

San Diego's Cedar Fire

The most serious fire was the Cedar Fire. It spread in just 1 day from Ramona to the San Diego city limits. Along the way it burned more than 200 square miles, or an area about the size of Chicago. Sadly, firefighters were unable to stop or even slow the fire immediately. One problem was a shortage of workers and equipment.

Usually during a large fire, a local fire department receives help from other departments in neighboring towns. However, that was impossible now. Too many **significant** fires were raging in Southern California at once. There was no assistance available. Each local engine company had to manage by itself.

Even some available fire engines had difficulty reaching the trouble spots. As the Cedar Fire spread, it jumped across highways and burned brush on both sides of the roads. Several major streets and highways had to be closed. All vehicles were brought to a halt, including many fire engines.

Many of the wildfires were unreachable—not only by ground but also by air. Often when a wildfire is difficult to reach by road, it is **preferable** to attack it first from the air. Firefighting airplanes and helicopters drop thousands of gallons of water on flames.

However, on the first night of the Cedar Fire, the U.S. Forest Service gave orders not to fly any planes or copters over the area. Officials were concerned because a thick blanket of smoke filled the air. They feared that aircraft might get lost in the dark smoke and crash.

In fact, on Sunday, October 26, a small private plane in San Diego County did crash while trying to land at a local airport. The pilot, blinded by smoke, missed the runway and smashed onto a highway. Fortunately, no one was seriously hurt. However, the plane burst into flames, adding to the fires already on the ground.

Bad Air

As fire and smoke continued to fill the air, the sky began to rain ash and soot. Breathing became difficult. Health officials warned people to stay indoors and keep their windows shut. The **peril** of breathing bad air was widespread. It affected **virtually** everyone in the region.

Many communities closed their schools and colleges. Some airports shut down, and numerous flights in and out of the state were cancelled. The courts closed. The mayor of San Diego asked employers to let their workers stay home on Monday, October 27.

People were not the only creatures kept indoors. At the San Diego Zoo, workers led many of the outdoor animals to safety inside zoo buildings. "Their lungs are built like ours," explained a staff member. "So they can be affected by the smoke."

Many people who went outside wore face masks. Drivers who dared to travel the roads used their headlights in midafternoon, due to the darkened, smoky conditions. One person said, "It was like the end of the world. You didn't feel like you were on Earth anymore."

You can see the smoke from the gigantic wildfires in this photograph taken by a satellite over Southern California. The orange areas show where the fires were burning.

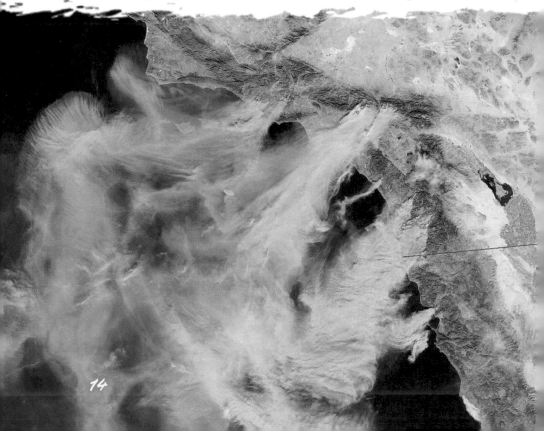

Lives Disrupted

Many public events had to be cancelled or relocated. A *Monday Night Football* game between the San Diego Chargers and the Miami Dolphins was moved from San Diego to Tempe, Arizona. City officials used the Chargers' stadium as an emergency shelter for fire victims driven from their homes.

In many Southern California communities, the police asked or ordered residents to leave their homes. Town officials turned schools and churches into evacuation shelters. Yet as the fires continued to spread, even some of those shelters had to be evacuated. Residents in Valley Center, California, had to relocate three times. First, they fled their homes for the Valley Center Middle School. Later, they **resumed** their evacuation, moving to the Valley Center High School. Finally, they settled in St. Peter's Catholic Church in Fallbrook.

In some places, citizens created their own shelters. At one large shopping center, the giant parking lot was turned into a community for mobile homes and other recreational vehicles. Some horse owners parked there with their trailers. Many walked their animals around the lot in an effort to calm them.

At each evacuation center, people coped as best they could. Some watched television or listened to radios for news about the fires. Others shared their stories about leaving their homes when the fires began. Where weather permitted, some kids even played a game of football.

Mostly, however, people in the shelters waited anxiously as the fires raged on. Many residents became filled with **skepticism**. As more time passed, some began to doubt that their homes were even still standing.

Battling the Blazes

As the wildfires raged, firefighting crews tried to meet each one head-on to stop it from spreading. Their jobs were not easy. In most cases, workers couldn't predict exactly how a fire would travel, where it would turn next. The flames, **induced** by the shifting Santa Ana winds, kept switching direction. San Diego's fire chief said of the Cedar Fire, "It changes with the wind direction, and the wind is created by the fire itself."

As blazes leaped across highways, they raced faster than fire crews could chase them. In San Bernardino County, two blazes—the Old Fire and the Grand Prix Fire—moved toward each other. When the two fires originated, they were 10 miles apart. After just 1 day, however, they merged into one gigantic blaze. Once the fire reached Los Angeles County, part of it broke away to start a new blaze that was called the Padua Fire.

Fire officials now feared that other wildfires might either merge or break away to cause even greater problems for firefighters. Additional crews and equipment were desperately needed to battle the growing blazes.

On Monday, October 27, California governor Gray Davis **intervened** in the crisis. He ordered 60 fire engines from other parts of the state. He also brought in 50 fire engines from Nevada and 25 fire engines from Arizona. In addition, the California National Guard provided more helicopters and airplanes to fight the fires by air.

Attacks from the air are extremely important, especially for wildfires that cannot be reached immediately by ground. Whenever the smoky skies permitted, firefighting planes called air tankers flew over the burning areas. They dropped massive amounts of water on the flames. Each plane holds up to 3,000 gallons of water.

16

An air tanker drops a fire retardant over the area.

Other air tankers dropped a fire retardant on the blazes. It is a substance that helps to slow and stop the spread of a fire. Fire retardant contains a pink dye that allows pilots and firefighters to see exactly where the retardant lands on the ground.

Helicopters also provided **significant** assistance in the air attacks. The copters made countless trips called bucket drops. Each copter would fly to a nearby lake or river and scoop several hundred gallons of water into a bucket that dangled from long ropes. Then, the pilot would fly over a fire area and release the water. The pilot would immediately return to the lake or river and repeat the entire process.

The air attacks were extremely difficult and dangerous. Thick smoke and ash in the sky made it **virtually** impossible for pilots to see clearly. The pilots also struggled to keep their planes and copters steady as the **vigorous** Santa Ana winds rocked aircraft. Soaring tree branches and other flying debris destroyed the windshields of six planes that flew over the blazing forests.

Smoke Jumpers and Hotshots

Where firefighters were able, they attacked a wildfire both by ground and by air. First, came the smoke jumpers. They are specially trained crews who parachute from airplanes into a blazing trouble spot. In Southern California, each team dropped into a region that was difficult for ground crews to reach immediately. The smoke jumpers were able to land exactly in a desired location. They avoided being blown off-course into sharp rocks, rivers, or the fire itself.

Next, came the hotshots. They are experienced firefighting teams who approach a wildfire by fire engine or on foot. Like the smoke jumpers, the hotshots have to be extremely careful when making their way toward a fire. In many parts of Southern California, the land is steep and rocky. Walking on bumpy ground while carrying up to 50 pounds of firefighting equipment can be a **perilous** task.

Once in position, both the smoke jumpers and hotshots performed the same basic jobs. First, they dug a fireline, or firebreak, around a blaze. A fireline is a wide, open path from which all burnable material is cleared away.

Work crews used special tools to clear away all burnable material in a fire's path.

The purpose of the fireline is to deprive the fire of the fuel it needs to keep spreading. Workers made the path as long as possible. The best kind of fireline completely surrounds a blaze.

Day after day, crewmembers used chain saws and axes to clear away all trees and brush within a fireline. A typical path, when completed, could be several miles long. It might also be anywhere from a few feet to several hundred feet wide.

Next, ground crews used shovels and other special tools to clear away logs, branches, leaves, and other litter that lay along the fireline. One tool they used was a Pulaski—a sharp, long-handled instrument. It has an axe on one side of the blade and a hoe on the other. Workers also used a McLeod—a tool that doubles as both a rake and a hoe.

At each site, firefighters worked as quickly as possible to complete their fireline. They cleared away all burnable material—even some of the soil. The result was a wide dirt path that ran around a wildfire. Nothing within the path could now burn.

Digging the fireline was only the first part of the job, however. Next, work crews purposely set their own fire, called a backfire. It burned all the ground between the fireline and the approaching wildfire. The purpose is to rid the area of all remaining burnable material. That way, when a wildfire meets a backfire, the two fires will have no more fuel to keep burning and will die out.

All during the last week of October, ground crews across Southern California **strived** bravely to create firelines and backfires. Team members worked up to 18 hours a day, digging and clearing away trees and brush. They were exhausted, yet the smoke jumpers and hotshots never gave up hope as they performed a seemingly impossible task. Somehow, they remained hopeful that they would soon tame the raging blazes.

Chapter 4

Tales of Heroism

If you were a firefighter, how far would you go to perform your duties? Would you work your required shift and then call it quits? Would you be willing to **strive** to work more than that, after your official workday is over?

One Southern California firefighter who showed true job dedication is Eric Brue. He is a member of the Los Angeles Fire Department. On a day when the Cedar Fire spread **extensively**, Brue was supposed to be off from work. However, he was unable to **justify** relaxing at home, knowing that other people were suffering. He felt he had to help.

Brue decided to spend his day off assisting the Miramar Fire Department, where he had once worked. However, he was unable to get there due to traffic jams caused by the fires. Instead he drove on side roads until reaching Scripps Ranch. There, he saw several homes in danger of burning. No other firefighters were around to help.

Brue spent the day trying to help save many residences, **alternating** among "18 houses with no water," as he later described it. His 14 years of firefighting experience came in handy. With just a chain saw and some garden tools, he dug firelines and kept the flames away from 16 of the 18 homes. Scripps Ranch residents praised Brue as a brave hero who risked his own safety to protect the property of others.

All across Southern California, other firefighters were doing the same thing. There was no **disputing** their dedication. By now, ground crews were suffering what is called firefighter fatigue. Many of the firefighters had worked long shifts, with little or no sleep. Yet these devoted individuals continued to do all they could to save people's lives and property. Despite a shortage of help, they fought what one firefighter called "house-to-house combat."

Tom Ridge, the secretary of homeland security, toured a fire area in Claremont, California. Afterward he told reporters, "I just met a fireman who was trying to save somebody else's house when his went up in flames. In the operations center, there are a couple of people on duty today—12-hour shifts. They lost their homes, but they know that they still have a job to do, and maybe their presence will help save somebody else's home."

Respect Is Required

As firefighters demonstrated their bravery, they also showed sensitivity and respect. Near La Jolla, California, the Paradise Fire burned through a Native American reservation. The land contains sites that are considered holy to the Native Americans who live there.

Elders of the La Jolla reservation met with fire officials and showed them the holy places to avoid. The firefighters were sensitive to the concerns of the Native American elders. As fire crews plowed bulldozers across land to create firelines, they respectfully bypassed those sacred spots. Tribal members were very grateful for the special consideration that the firefighters showed.

"Our job isn't just protecting homes and people," explained a member of the California Department of Forestry. "It's also protecting all the other resources out there."

Firefighters did their best to protect the homes of Southern California residents during the wildfires.

Ordinary Heroes

Firefighters weren't always able to protect homes and other property by themselves. In many cases, they teamed up with local citizens who proved that they, too, could be heroes in a fire crisis. In one community, former firefighter Steve Ritchie worked with two neighbors, Wills Booth and Brian Duffy. The trio saved a dozen homes from the Cedar Fire. They used Booth's own fire engine and water pump truck to hose down flames while also spraying houses with fire-resistant foam.

Ritchie, Booth, and Duffy took on an especially dangerous job. Their community, like many others in the region, was next to rugged wild lands. A fire in this kind of region is called an intermix fire, because it involves both wild lands and building materials. It is the worst kind of fire to battle. An intermix fire occurs in areas where clusters of new wood-frame houses are built close to uncleared vegetation, such as forests. Wild lands are prone to wildfires, which puts these neighborhoods at risk as well.

Besides the closeness to wild land, there were other problems to face. Roads to and from the neighborhood are narrow and twisting. Often they lead to dead ends in canyons. With no alternate exit, firefighters can find themselves cornered by flames. Fortunately, Ritchie, Booth, and Duffy received help from Chris Cornette, a captain with the California Department of Forestry. He owned one of the 12 homes at risk. Cornette and five other men dug firelines and set backfires in the canyon. As they worked, strong winds blew the wildfire over a ridge toward Booth's home. From Tuesday afternoon until Thursday night, Booth, Duffie, and Ritchie battled flames that sometimes rose 100 feet into the air.

"I looked at them and they were engulfed in [surrounded by] flames," Cornette recalled later, describing the houses. "It was a recipe for death." Fortunately, everyone involved survived. Thanks to their heroic efforts, all 12 homes were unharmed.

Sometimes residents had no help at all from firefighters. As the Cedar Fire raced toward one Ramona neighborhood, 20 people there prepared for battle. Early Sunday morning, they began to clear the land with bulldozers. Police officers visited and warned residents to evacuate. However, nearly everyone **preferred** to stay put. One bulldozer driver was almost 80 years old. "Boys," he told officers, "I got some dozer work to do."

Neighbors cleared a 50-foot-wide fireline that stretched for several miles. When the fire finally arrived, residents pumped well water and sprayed garden hoses to douse the flames. They worked from Sunday to Wednesday, pumping about 60,000 gallons of water in all. Without **dispute**, their efforts paid off. In the end, everything on one side of the fireline was burned. Yet everything on the other side of the fireline was saved, including farms and houses. With no professional help, residents had saved **virtually** their entire community.

Saving Lives

If you have ever been rescued from a fire, you can fully understand and appreciate the value of firefighters. They are famous for their courage on the job. Their reputation is certainly **justified**. Firefighters risk their lives to save people whom they have never met.

Two heroes in the Cedar Fire were Matt Buzzell and Scott Fenton. They are Lakeside firefighting paramedics who received a call on Sunday afternoon that a woman was trapped inside her home in Alpine. The men arrived at the house and heard a woman screaming inside.

"It was high-pitched, life-threatening—an urgent call," recalled Fenton. He broke through the front door of the house, with Buzzell right behind him. Inside, thick smoke filled the living room. The two men were able to spot the woman. They immediately pulled her outside.

Just then, more help arrived. San Miguel battalion chief Andy Menshek and paramedic Modesto Martinez came to the house. They were congratulating Buzzell and Fenton on their good job. Suddenly, the woman made a surprising announcement: Her husband was still inside the house!

Menshek acted immediately. Taking a deep breath, he entered the house. By now, it was entirely wrapped in flames, and gas tanks were exploding. Unfortunately, Menshek had to retreat due to extreme heat and smoke.

"Did you save my husband?" the woman asked.

"We're not going to lose this guy," Menshek promised.

He grabbed his flashlight and re-entered the house with Martinez. Smoke was pouring through the burned-out house. The men knew it was dangerous to **resume** their rescue effort but willingly took the risk. They crawled on the floor about 20 feet. Suddenly, the flashlight revealed a man's leg right ahead of them.

Firefighters rescued victims who were trapped or injured by flames.

Through the smoke, Menshek and Martinez saw the outline of an older man leaning over his walker. Later, Martinez said, "I could see some embers and smoke coming from his back where he had been burned."

The two rescuers dragged the man outside while hot flames licked dangerously at their legs. Trees were burning all around them. The firefighters placed both the husband and wife, along with their dog, in an ambulance. They drove them to a nearby building, where the victims were then placed into a medical helicopter. The firefighters felt good about their rescue but had no time to relax. Immediately after the incident, they received orders to protect other homes in Alpine.

Later, Chief Menshek said, "This kind of rescue takes some of the sadness away from the lives that have been lost and the homes that have been destroyed." He then turned to his men, shook their hands, and said proudly, "Nice job, guys."

Animals Rescued

The elderly husband and wife rescued by Menshek and Martinez were lucky to be saved and to have their dog saved as well. In their rescue efforts, firefighters saved more than human lives; they also saved the lives of many animals. Bill Hurd, a Julian volunteer firefighter, heard about the Cedar Fire approaching the California Wolf Center on Monday night. Twenty-nine wolves were trapped inside the building. Hurd and a group of volunteers from the center desperately battled the blazes.

As hot embers fell from the sky, Hurd and the other workers hosed down the area. The police, **skeptical** about their safety, evacuated everyone at midnight. Only Hurd stayed behind to fight the blazes all night.

When the fire finally **subsided**, Hurd was tired and completely covered in gray ash and black soot but victorious. He had saved all 29 wolves. Animal lovers everywhere hailed Hurd as a hero. Yet he responded modestly, saying, "I had no choice but to do what I did."

The Ultimate Sacrifice

Tragically, one firefighter lost his life in the California wildfires of 2003. He was 38-year-old Steven Rucker, a member of the Novato Fire Protection District in Northern California. He died on Wednesday, October 29, while battling the Cedar Fire in Wynola, a town west of Julian. He and his team had arrived the day before to help the local firefighters.

As the fire neared several homes, it burned unpredictably, **induced** by the strong Santa Ana winds. In one unexpected shift, the flames suddenly leaped at Rucker and others in his crew. Unfortunately, Rucker was killed and three other firefighters were injured in the blaze. Fire captain Doug McDonald received serious burns. Shawn Kreps, a fire engineer, and Barrett Smith, a paramedic, suffered minor burns. They were flown to a hospital burn unit near San Diego for treatment.

Word of Rucker's death spread quickly. Firefighters across California were saddened by the tragic news. Rucker was an 11-year veteran who left behind a wife and two children.

"When one of us dies, it affects us all," said a volunteer firefighter from Mount Laguna. "But we can't let our emotions get in the way."

John Hawkins of the California Department of Forestry called Rucker's sacrifice "an example of the American spirit of protecting our assets." He added, "Steve Rucker gave his life today in pursuit of saving someone else's house." Hawkins further praised Rucker by saying, "He stood the test. He stood tall." No one could **dispute** that tribute.

On Thursday, October 30, firefighters all across California honored Rucker in a moment of silence. They lowered flags outside all fire stations in the state to half-mast in Rucker's memory. In addition, firefighters attached black tape to their badges and fire engines. These symbolic gestures were a grim reminder to firefighters of the extreme dangers they faced. They reminded all Californians of the dedication and spirit that firefighters everywhere possess.

Firefighters remembered their crewmember Steven Rucker, who lost his life in the Southern California wildfires of 2003.

Chapter 5

Victory at Last

Imagine stepping inside the boots of a firefighter in Southern California in October of 2003. You've been battling raging wildfires **virtually** nonstop for more than a week. You feel tired and overwhelmed each time you **resume** the struggle. Yet you haven't abandoned hope. With more time and a little luck, you will finally be able to control the blazes and extinguish them for good.

That's exactly how firefighters across Southern California felt as October came to an end. They had been waging a losing battle against uncontrollable blazes. Yet they were determined to continue the struggle until conditions turned in their favor.

Governor Davis again **intervened** by ordering additional work crews to the fire areas. By Thursday, October 30, a total of about 13,000 firefighters were **vigorously** battling the blazes across the region. The governor praised the firefighters. He said, "They are standing up to the worst of Mother Nature and, in so doing, they represent California's very best." He added, "We will never forget these firefighters. We will never forget these people who...defend our homes, our businesses, our lives."

Sharing the Work

Both professionals and volunteers participated in fighting the fires. The military assisted, too. The U.S. Army trained and sent 500 marines from Camp Pendleton to help battle the blazes. In addition, the Marine Corps made six more helicopters available for water drops. The pilots had spent several days learning how to guide their crafts in hot, windy conditions.

Not all those who joined in the struggle were even Americans. Fifteen trained firefighters from Mexico traveled north to help battle the Cedar Fire. One grateful California resident said, "It just couldn't be more fantastic for people from Mexico to be helping us. They certainly have big hearts."

The Weather Shifts

Finally, on that Thursday morning, firefighters received some **significant** and long-awaited relief—a change in the weather. The air, which had previously been hot and dry, turned cool and moist. Rain began to fall. On Palomar Mountain, light fog and drizzle weakened the fires. The weather, along with increased air and ground attacks, finally began to slow the raging blazes. "At this point, the weather is helping," said Alameda County fire captain Randy Moore. "The fire is lying down."

Residents of Julian, California, were especially uplifted by the change. It was near their town where firefighter Steve Rucker had lost his life in the Cedar Fire just a day earlier. They knew that Thursday's cooler weather would now give firefighters a better chance to contain and control the blazes.

As the weather changed, so did fire officials' plan of attack. Until now, firefighters had **strived** mainly to protect the homes in wild-land communities and neighborhoods. Now, the battle switched to the open fields. Work crews could focus more on surrounding and weakening the fires than on defending homes. In short, their fight became offensive instead of defensive.

By that Thursday, firefighting was also made easier because so much vegetation had already burned. There was now much less brush to feed the flames.

The arrival of rain and cold weather gave exhausted firefighters a chance to catch up on badly needed sleep.

"We're at the point now where we can almost see the end of the fires," said a spokesperson for the California Department of Forestry.

On that same day, San Diego city employees returned to work. The courts reopened, and citizens were ordered to report for jury duty. Classes **resumed** at all colleges in the region. Elementary schools remained closed, however. Health officials said it was **preferable** for young children to stay indoors and limit their exercise because the poor air quality might still pose a risk for them. Some day-care centers opened on Thursday, but children were kept indoors.

That night, additional rain fell in San Diego County. It dampened even more of the flames that had once raged across the region. By Friday, the Cedar Fire—the largest of all the wildfires—was 65 percent contained, or surrounded. Two days earlier, it had been only 15 percent contained. Significant progress was being made.

Cooling Off

By Friday night, October 31, the spirit of Southern Californians was high. In San Diego, businesses organized Halloween parties for children whose families had been forced to evacuate their homes. The most popular costume was a firefighter outfit. It reflected the pride that everyone took in the brave professionals who protected their property and lives.

The next day brought a new month and new progress in the fire battles. Wildfires continued to **subside**, thanks to even damper, colder weather. The temperature on Mount Laguna dropped to about 48 degrees Fahrenheit.

"The cooler temperatures, the rainfall, and the increase in the humidity definitely have helped the firefighters," said Brad Doyle, a forecaster for the National Weather Service.

The Cedar Fire was now 81 percent contained. Forestry officials predicted it would be completely contained by Monday, November 3. Indeed, they were correct. As a result, many tired firefighters from around California received permission to return home. Some 300 fire engines and their crews went back to their own cities. Many local firefighters were also able to relax. "I'm looking forward to taking a hot shower and sleeping in my own bed," sighed a firefighter from Hanford, California.

Not everyone was able to quit, however. Some firefighters remained to cope with small fires still burning. They walked through the brush, searching for hot spots that might suddenly flare up. "This is a critical time to make sure we complete the job," said Michael Lohrey, a fire commander with the U.S. Forest Service. For the most part, however, the wildfires had finally been defeated.

Chapter 6

Loss and Recovery

By Monday, November 3, 2003, the wildfire crisis was nearly over. It had **originated** 2 weeks earlier, when the first two wildfires flared up on October 21. Now each of the 11 fires was either completely or almost completely contained.

Southern Californians were relieved that the fires had finally **subsided**. Yet their relief was mixed with shock, sadness, anger, and disbelief upon seeing the **extensive** damage that had occurred. Much of the destroyed land is in mountain and canyon communities, where about 3,400 homes burned to the ground. Losses totaled more than $2 billion. Most tragically, 20 people—including one firefighter—lost their lives as a result of the fires. In addition, thousands of animals perished, including several hundred cattle.

The losses were overwhelming and often hard to imagine. In some cases, entire towns were **virtually** wiped out. The community of Cuyamaca was "totally destroyed," according to Bill Clayton, division chief of the California Department of Forestry. Nearly all of its 145 homes were lost in the Cedar Fire.

Popular vacation spots and resorts were also destroyed, with living quarters and restaurants going up in flames. Entire campgrounds were burned out and are now completely unusable.

Among the hardest hit fire areas were 14 Native American reservations. Thousands of acres of land burned, and scores of homes are now gone. Reservations made up about 29,000 acres, or nearly 10 percent of all land destroyed by the Cedar and Paradise Fires. Ironically, the Viejas Indian Reservation did not burn as much as other reservations because cattle had already eaten much of the grass there before the fires arrived. "This week we were grateful for them," said one tribal member.

People who had been living in shelters or with family or friends during the fires were now anxious to see what, if anything, remained of their homes. However, many residents were not allowed to return to their houses immediately. Fire officials first had to check on the physical condition of each residence. People could not go back in until officials could guarantee the safety of their structure.

A Summary of the Fires

Fire	County	Began	Acres Burned
Camp Pendleton	San Diego	October 21	9,000
Grand Prix	San Bernardino	October 21	59,448
Piru	Ventura	October 23	64,000
Verdale	Los Angeles	October 24	8,680
Cedar	San Diego	October 25	280,293
Old	San Bernardino	October 25	91,281
Simi	Simi Valley, Ventura, Los Angeles	October 25	108,204
Dulzura	San Diego	October 26	45,971
Paradise	San Diego	October 26	56,700
Mountain	Riverside	October 26	10,331
Padua	Los Angeles	October 27	10,466

When fire victims finally did return home, many found only worthless piles of ashes. One homeowner couldn't believe her eyes. "The fire must have been so intense," she said, stunned. "It took the aluminum and turned it into a puddle."

The losses were heartbreaking to individuals and their families. People lost letters and photographs, for example. Imagine if you could not replace items that were valuable to you. Some objects that are expensive, such as cars or appliances, can be replaced. Other meaningful possessions, such as home videos and old family photographs, cannot.

Even with people back in their homes, the effects of the fires were sorely felt. Some blazes had knocked out electrical power lines belonging to the San Diego Gas and Electric Company. While the fires were raging, the company had sent out hundreds of work crews to repair 1,500 burned poles, thousands of miles of damaged power lines, and other necessary equipment. Now, even after the fires were out, tens of thousands of homes and offices were still without electricity or gas.

Even people who never had to evacuate their homes, or who lived outside the fire areas, suffered from the effects of the fires. When the blazes spread, fire officials asked those residents to cut back on their water use so firefighters would have more water available. Many went without electrical and telephone service for a week or more until repairs could be made.

Numerous cell phones also did not work. The company American Telephone and Telegraph (AT&T) reported that the fires had damaged many of its cellular sites. The problem grew worse because residents in Southern California made more calls than usual during the fires and after they ended. The huge number of calls jammed those sites that were working.

The quality of drinking water was also poor because soot had fallen into lakes and rivers. In many communities, health officials told residents it was **preferable** to boil their tap water before drinking it. School children received bottled water as a safety precaution.

The Mudslide Crisis

Across Southern California, the most obvious sign of fire loss was the burned vegetation in the countryside. Millions of trees and plants in mountains and valleys were reduced to ashes. That would have been damaging enough. However, the extensive loss of vegetation, combined with the recent rainfall, created a new problem for people in the wild lands: mudslides.

A mudslide is similar to a landslide or snow avalanche. It occurs when muddy ground on the side of a steep hill or mountain suddenly gives way and tumbles down the slope. Ordinarily, the roots of trees and plants in the soil help the ground remain solid and steady. However, after the wildfires wiped out so much vegetation, the land lacked nature's protection against mudslides.

One mudslide occurred on November 1, even before the fires were out. It happened in the town of Crestline after an inch of rain fell on the region. Mud suddenly came rushing down a hillside and blocked the area's main highway. It was difficult for firefighters to **intervene** in this type of situation.

A much worse **peril** occurred nearly 2 months later, in late December. Heavy rain fell on the San Bernardino Mountains. It **induced** a mudslide in Waterman Canyon that killed 16 people who were camping there. Clearly, the Southern California wildfires were still able to bring death and destruction, even months after they had been extinguished.

Rebuilding Lives

"We'll plan our attack and get back on our feet." That's the note that one restaurant owner left on his front door for residents of Cuyamaca after a wildfire destroyed most of their town. All across Southern California, fire victims adopted the same optimistic attitude. They knew they couldn't just sit and mourn their losses. They had no **alternative** but to begin the task of rebuilding their homes and lives.

The lucky ones had homes left to return to. Jolene and Michael Crowley had nearly completed remodeling their San Diego County home when the fires forced them to evacuate. They had just repainted the outside of the house and installed a new marble tile fireplace. Returning home after the fire, the Crowleys found that the fireplace was badly damaged. The heat of the flames had melted pairs of marble tiles together. Yet Jolene Crowley refused to be discouraged. She showed a visitor a pile of marble tiles that had been piled outdoors. "Isn't it pretty?" she asked, smiling.

Michael Crowley had recently converted a shed in the backyard into a library. There had been 27 crates of books in the shed when the fire struck. In spite of the extensive destruction to the books, Crowley, a criminal lawyer, managed to see some humor in the situation. "What's really funny," he noted, "was that just last week I paid a company $150 to shred years of clients' files. If I'd just waited..."

The Crowleys **preferred** to rebuild their badly damaged house instead of moving somewhere else. They couldn't bear the thought of leaving nearby friends and neighbors. "I'm thinking about the opportunity," Michael Crowley said. "I have to go into action." Later, pondering how lucky he was just to be alive, he observed, "It puts all your little problems in perspective."

Cleaning Up

Residents who moved back into their homes found there was much work to do. First, they called representatives of insurance companies and government relief agencies, who visited their homes to evaluate the damage. Next, residents called carting companies to haul away burned debris. Then, they made plans to rebuild their houses. In addition, ranchers with dead cattle on their land had to bury their animals.

Think about the kind of work it would take to get a home cleaned up after a terrible fire. What would you have to do? One of the most rigorous tasks for homeowners was removing the soot and ash that now blanketed their property. Here are some cleaning tips that health officials offered:

- ✔ Hose away ash and soot into lawns, not down city storm drains. Otherwise, the drains could clog and cause flooding during a rainfall.
- ✔ Don't use leaf blowers to clear away ash and soot. Wet the debris and then scrape or sweep it away.
- ✔ Wash your car at a carwash or over a grassy area such as your lawn.
- ✔ Use damp cloths to pick up dust from tables, floors, and other hard surfaces.
- ✔ Change your furnace filter so it doesn't blow dirt when you use it.

Residents had plenty of cleaning to do once the fires stopped burning.

All Kinds of Help

Most fire victims relied on family, friends, and neighbors to help them get their lives back in order. Sometimes that meant moving in with them until the victims' homes could be rebuilt or repaired. Strangers volunteered, too. Thousands of Americans sent food, clothes, and money to relief organizations such as the American Red Cross. Alex Spanos, owner of the San Diego Chargers football team, donated $1 million to fire victims. "We can't replace a lifetime of memories, but hopefully, in some small way, we can help people get back on their feet," Spanos said.

The spirit of generosity spread throughout Southern California. In Alpine, Postal Annex, a postal services retail chain store, offered fire victims free mailboxes for 6 months while the victims were kept from their homes. At a fire station in Valley Center, residents stopped by to bring home-cooked meals to firefighters. It was a sign that the firefighters' bravery had not been forgotten.

Government Aid

Local, state, and federal governments also assisted fire victims greatly. During the wildfires, President George W. Bush had visited Southern California and declared the affected counties to be disaster areas. That meant that people who suffered losses in the fire could receive government money to help them recover.

The government set up a number of relief centers where victims could apply for assistance. Officials showed them how to file for grants, loans, and other aid. Both the federal government and the state of California provided millions of dollars to help victims, including people who now needed housing, transportation, or jobs.

In addition, special teams of government investigators visited residents of the burned-out communities. They tried to prevent building contractors without licenses from doing home repairs for victims. The government wanted to make sure that nobody took advantage of the victims of the fires.

Conclusion: The Fires Next Time

History indicates that the wildfires of 2003 will not be Southern California's last. Wildfires are an annual occurrence there. In fact, some experts predict that global warming will increase the number of fires in the future. They say hotter, drier, windier weather will **induce** even worse fires.

So what can be done now to protect people and property from the next fire? Experts say one solution is to stop individuals from building homes so close to areas with thick vegetation. In some places, such laws already exist. In Ventura County, a law requires a 100-foot buffer zone between homes and nearby wild lands. People should look **skeptically** at sites before they build new homes. Homeowners also benefit by having brick patios, gravel walkways, and swimming pools. They are useful firelines that deprive a fire of fuel and stop it from traveling.

In addition, the number of trees that feed the fires in forests must be reduced. Congress has already passed a new law that encourages "thinning"—the cutting of extra trees. The Healthy Forests Restoration Act allows the thinning of trees on 20 million acres of U.S. forests, many in California. Perhaps, if these measures are taken, tragic losses like the ones in 2003 will never occur again.

WILD
Winds

How Tornadoes Start, and What They Do

by Amy Jolin

The devastating tornado of March 18, 1925, would have looked much like this one.

CHAPTER 1

A Twister's Coming!

March 17, 1925, was hot and muggy in eastern Missouri. People sat under shade trees and wished for a breath of wind. If only a little rain would fall from the sky, they might get some relief from the heat.

These people got their wish for wind and rain in an unexpected way. To the south and west, a huge mass of heavy, wet air had just slammed into another large mass of air that had moved down from the north. Together, this air was blowing toward Missouri, and fast!

By morning on March 18, the sky was cloudy. By midday, it was black with heavy, dark clouds that blocked the sun. By 1:00 p.m., the wind had whipped into a massive tornado that touched down in Reynolds County, Missouri. It ripped through the countryside, tearing a path **approximately** three-quarters of a mile wide. The force of the wind pulled up trees and knocked over houses. By the time the tornado reached the Mississippi River, it had grown into a massive storm.

A man named F. M. Hewitt saw the tornado hit DeSoto, Illinois. He described the sky as "a seething, boiling mass of clouds whose color constantly changed. From the upper portion came a roaring noise [like that] of many trains." During a flash of lightning, Hewitt watched a house nearby explode as if it had been blasted with dynamite.

This massive storm would be called the Tri-State Tornado. It traveled across Missouri, Illinois, and Indiana at a rate of 60 miles per hour and covered 219 miles in just under 4 hours, destroying parts of all three states. It is still ranked as one of the nation's worst tornado disasters.

The Tri-State Tornado happened before scientists had developed ways of **detecting** and predicting tornadoes. In 1925, few scientists had studied the reasons why tornadoes form. They had no idea how to tell when a tornado would be born or where it would go. Also, in 1925, most people had no warnings about tornadoes. People listened to the radio, but they did not get regular weather reports as we do today. In contrast, today weather scientists, called meteorologists, study tornadoes closely. They know the weather conditions that are right for the formation of tornadoes.

In this book, you will read about how tornadoes form and the terrible damage they can cause. You will also read about some of the warning systems that people use when a tornado is **inevitable**. You will see why it is rare today for hundreds of people to be killed by a tornado in the United States—even by one as big as the Tri-State Tornado.

To understand how tornadoes form, you need to know what causes wind. In the next chapter, you will read about how and why wind blows. You will also learn how blowing winds turn into storms—storms fierce enough to breed tornadoes.

CHAPTER 2

Wind

Wind is air that is moving. We cannot see it, but we can judge how fast it is moving by the effect that it has on objects. The movement of air as it passes over Earth can determine whether a storm system will form.

What causes wind? When the Sun heats the air, the warm air rises away from the ground. As the warm air ascends, cooler air moves in to take its place. We feel the air movement as wind.

Why does warm air rise and cold air sink? Cold air is heavier than warm air. If that sounds **irrational** to you, think about being in a big house on a hot day. Where would you rather be: in the attic, or the cellar? Because heavier, cold air sinks down, and lighter, warm air rises, the cellar would be a much cooler place. In fact, upstairs rooms in a home can be 6 to 10 degrees warmer and basements 6 to 10 degrees cooler than ground-level rooms.

Scientists recorded the eerie sounds made by this tornado's winds.

What happens when masses of warm, moist air meet dense, cold air? Huge clouds build up at the point where these air masses are struggling for position. The tops are often bright white with sunshine, whereas the bottoms are usually dark and heavy, with an **aggressive**, threatening appearance. A thunderstorm forms.

Sometimes, a thunderstorm develops into a powerful type of storm called a supercell. This storm is different from other storms. It can last for hours and travel for hundreds of miles. It can produce sudden floods of rain and hail the size of baseballs. Hail that big can damage cars and houses and hurt people and animals.

A supercell is caused when a stream of warm, moist air rises up through a storm. This stream is called an updraft. Wind blowing through the storm from different directions can make the updraft rotate. So far, the supercell is still a thunderstorm. However, if a strong wind blows down through the storm, a narrow, rotating column of air called a funnel can develop. A funnel that reaches all the way from the thundercloud to the ground is a tornado.

Measuring Winds

How do meteorologists measure the winds that create such large storm systems? There are two basic measurements for describing wind: wind direction and wind speed. To measure the direction of wind, a person tells where the wind is coming from. For example, if there is a north wind blowing, that means the wind is coming from someplace north of the **site** from which it is being measured.

Wind speed is measured in miles per hour. Meteorologists use special instruments, such as a wind vane or an anemometer, that record wind speed and determine wind direction.

Tornado Winds

The winds of a tornado can play amazing tricks. For example, some tornado winds have been known to pluck all the feathers off a chicken. Others have driven tiny pieces of straw directly into solid wood. In one case, a plank of wood was driven into the side of a tree. The plank wedged there so tightly that a grown man could stand on its free end.

All tornadoes are violent and destructive windstorms. Some tornadoes, though, are more destructive than others. Tornado damage is **primarily** caused by fast, powerful wind and flying objects rather than by rain or lightning. Just how fast is the wind in a tornado? That question is hard to answer. Most wind instruments are destroyed by the fierce winds of a tornado. Even if an instrument could stand up to the wind, no one can tell where to place the tool to make sure to get it in a tornado's path.

Strong tornado winds can cause unusual incidents, such as a wooden plank smashing through a windshield.

Many scientists have tried to develop devices to learn more about the wind speed inside tornadoes. In the 1980s, scientists tried launching helium balloons into tornadoes. These balloons were supposed to take little sensors up to the clouds and measure wind speed and air pressure, sending back radio waves of data. The balloons had to be released directly into a storm. They worked sometimes, but they needed constant **adjustments**. Sometimes the balloons were not able to lift the instruments off the ground. At other times, they would burst or quickly rise above the storm.

Today, scientists use a type of radar called Doppler radar to predict when tornadoes may form. The radar used by police officers measures the speed of moving cars. Doppler radar measures the speed of moving raindrops. Special computers **detect** how fast the wind is blowing rain under a cloud or within a tornado. Doppler radar also tells how quickly a storm cloud is moving. In 1988, scientists set up a huge network of Doppler radar stations called NEXRAD, which stands for *nex*t generation *rada*r. This system looks for weather patterns every hour of every day.

Doppler radar cannot determine when or where a tornado will form. This type of radar can only tell where the wind and clouds are forming that may produce a tornado. However, the Doppler radar system is still the safest and most accurate method of predicting tornadoes in the United States today.

Doppler radar is useful for predicting the conditions for a tornado, but the actual wind speed is still difficult to measure. A scientist named T. Theodore Fujita developed a scale that measures a tornado not by wind speed, but by the amount of destruction caused by the wind. This scale is called the Fujita scale, or F-scale for short. Fujita tried to estimate the possible wind speeds that could cause such damage.

Fujita Tornado Damage Scale

Scale	Wind Estimate (miles per hour)	Typical Damage
F0	less than 73	**Light Damage** Wind damages chimneys and signboards; branches are broken off trees; trees with shallow roots are pushed over.
F1	73–112	**Moderate Damage** Wind peels the surface off roofs; mobile homes are pushed off their foundations or overturned; moving cars are blown off roads.
F2	113–157	**Considerable Damage** Roofs are torn off frame houses; mobile homes are destroyed; boxcars on trains are turned over; large trees are snapped or uprooted; light objects project forcefully, like missiles; cars are lifted off the ground.
F3	158–206	**Severe Damage** Roofs and some walls are torn off houses; trains are overturned; most trees in forests are uprooted; heavy cars are lifted off the ground and thrown.
F4	207–260	**Devastating Damage** Well-constructed houses are leveled; structures with weak foundations are blown some distance away; cars are thrown, and large objects project like missiles.
F5	261–318	**Incredible Damage** Strong frame houses are lifted off their foundations and swept away; objects the size of cars fly through the air farther than 100 yards; bark is ripped from trees; incredible phenomena occur.

Some of the descriptions on the F-scale talk about objects flying through the air. The wind in an F2 tornado can pick up loose objects such as lawn chairs or trash cans and blow them through the air with great force. In an F3 or F4 tornado, the wind can lift a heavy car right off the ground and throw it. The most extreme tornado, an F5, has winds that can top 300 miles per hour. These winds cause incredible damage. They can send an object the size of a car flying for more than 100 yards. It is in these tornadoes that the most unbelievable events occur.

The F-scale is a good measure of the destructive power of a tornado, but it does not measure the damage left by the tornado. For example, an F3 tornado that hits a big town can do much more damage to property and can kill many more people than an F5 tornado that strikes a country area where few people live. Of course, the most damaging tornadoes are those F5 tornadoes that strike major cities, leaving hundreds of people dead and destroying thousands of homes and buildings.

When you think of the damage that a tornado can do, it's hard to believe that about 800 tornadoes touch down in the United States every year. In fact, the majority of those tornadoes hit a part of the country that is known as Tornado Alley.

CHAPTER 3

Tornado Alley

When the first settlers moved to the Great Plains in the central United States, they had to make many **adjustments** in their lives. They discovered land and weather that many had never seen or heard of before. They experienced hot, dry summers and cold winters with blizzards that could last for days. They found vast stretches of flat prairie and wide-open skies. One of the unfortunate discoveries they made was the power of tornadoes.

Some people traveled from the eastern United States to settle the Great Plains. They came **primarily** from states where tornadoes rarely form. Other settlers traveled from Europe, a hilly and mountainous continent. European settlers had never seen a tornado either. Trees, mountains, and valleys can stop giant storm systems from forming. Out on the plains, though, the flat land offers no protection from big storms. Thunderstorms are common, and those storms can produce tornadoes.

The settlers were stunned by the awesome destruction of the tornadoes. Some could not believe that tornadoes existed until they saw one for themselves. As great tornadoes struck, some settlers believed that the world was about to end, and many were frightened away. However, the Plains settlers had a powerful **motive** for staying. The land was very fertile and good for farming.

Today, the Great Plains has so many tornadoes every year that a particular region has been nicknamed Tornado Alley. Tornado Alley stretches from central Texas north through South Dakota. An average of 700 tornadoes strike Tornado Alley every year. In fact, this area gets more tornadoes than anyplace else in the world.

How does this record compare in **proportion** to other parts of the United States? Tornadoes have hit all 50 of America's states at some time or another. Florida is one state that lies outside Tornado Alley but has many tornadoes every year. However, Florida's weather conditions are different from the ones that trigger severe thunderstorms in Tornado Alley. Tornadoes in Florida tend to be weaker.

Prevailing Westerlies

What causes Tornado Alley to have so many tornadoes? To answer that question, it helps to imagine that you are looking down at Earth from above the North Pole. You would see our planet spinning in a counterclockwise direction. In other words, the direction in which Earth rotates is the opposite of the way a clock's hands move around the clock. While the planet spins, hot air is rising from the equator and flowing toward the north pole. To people in the United States, this air movement feels as if the wind is always blowing from the west. These winds are called the prevailing westerlies.

Of course, anyone who ever went boating on a small lake would say that wind changes direction all the time. That fact is true on a small scale. On a large scale, however, scientists in the United States have measured many more winds blowing from the west than from any other direction.

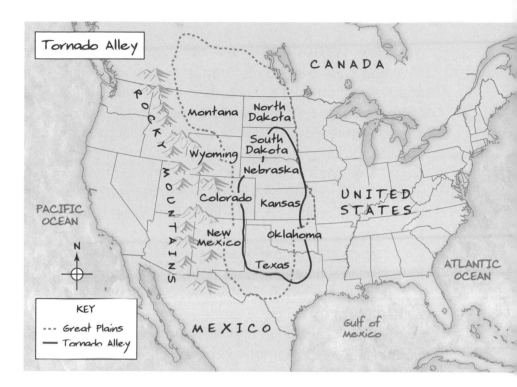

Tornado Alley

CANADA

Montana
North Dakota
South Dakota
Wyoming
Nebraska
Colorado
Kansas
New Mexico
Oklahoma
Texas

UNITED STATES

PACIFIC OCEAN

ROCKY MOUNTAINS

N

ATLANTIC OCEAN

MEXICO

Gulf of Mexico

KEY
- - - Great Plains
—— Tornado Alley

Breeding Ground for Tornadoes

Tornado Alley lies east of the Rocky Mountains. That means that westerly winds from the Pacific Ocean have to rise over the Rockies to get to Tornado Alley. As the wind rises, it cools and dumps rain. When the air gets to the top of the Rockies, it is high, dry, and cold.

South of Tornado Alley lies the Gulf of Mexico. Wind blows wet air that begins over this large body of water toward land. The sun heats the air. This warm, wet air blows north toward Tornado Alley.

The warm, wet air from the south floats close to the ground for a short period of time. Above it floats the cold, dry air that was over the mountains. Remember that cold air is heavier than warm air, and warm air rises. The trouble starts when cold, dry, heavy air begins smashing down on warm, wet air. The pressure can't last for long. Supercell thunderstorms can—and often do—result. These supercells can breed tornadoes.

Multiple Tornadoes

When supercell storms form, they can cause an outbreak of tornadoes. An outbreak is a series of tornadoes in the same area, coming from the same storm. Outbreaks can, and do, happen in states that lie outside Tornado Alley. However, the record for property damage belongs to an outbreak of tornadoes that struck Tornado Alley on May 3, 1999. More than 70 tornadoes hit parts of Oklahoma, Kansas, and Texas on this date.

Why was this outbreak so deadly? The tornadoes struck heavily populated areas. In Oklahoma, 44 people were killed on that day. In Kansas, tornadoes killed 5 people. Weather from the same storm system claimed another life in Texas on May 4. Hundreds more people were injured, and property damage cost about $1 billion. It was the costliest tornado damage in the history of the United States.

The death toll would have been worse without the warnings that reached citizens from many sources. People who lived in states in the path of the tornadoes heard warnings on every TV and radio station. Police drove up and down streets, telling residents to get to shelter. TV stations in Oklahoma City even stopped their regular broadcasting so they could cover the storm.

People who live in Tornado Alley are well aware of the dangers **represented** by the storms. They make special preparations to be sure that everyone knows how to react when severe weather arrives. For example, in Kansas, one week at the beginning of tornado season is called Severe Weather Awareness Week. Weather service workers stage two statewide tornado safety drills. In these drills, all citizens are asked to react as if there were real danger. The people in Kansas take the drills seriously.

CHAPTER 4

The Life of a Tornado

Although all tornadoes are formed from the meeting of air masses, no one tornado is the same as another. Tornadoes vary in size and shape, and in wind speed and intensity. They can occur during heavy rain and hail or without any precipitation at all.

Despite their many differences, tornadoes have some things in common. For example, tornadoes **primarily** occur when the sky is cloudy, although they are not always part of very big storms. The cloud that a tornado's funnel comes from is called its parent cloud.

Within the funnel is the sucking and swirling air that can suck up huge objects and lift them off the ground. This upward air motion at the center of the tornado is called the vortex. In the vortex, wind is rising at incredible speed. The vortex is the powerhouse of the tornado. If a tornado simply brushes the side of a building, it can blow off walls or siding. When the actual vortex strikes a house directly, the wind, rising at great speed, can lift the house from the ground!

A powerful vortex swirls inside this tornado's funnel.

Debris Clouds

Most wind is invisible. At the same time, it is true that a tornado can appear to a viewer to be black, gray, blue, white, or even red. There is a **rational** explanation for this. At the point where many tornadoes touch the ground, they create something called a debris cloud. From a distance, it looks like a dark cloud near the ground. In fact, the cloud is made of dirt, garbage, stones, and any other scrap, or debris, the wind has picked up. As a tornado destroys homes or objects in its path, the debris cloud becomes bigger and more dangerous.

It is partly this debris that gives a tornado its color. How does this work?

The debris cloud of a tornado can be made up of anything, from dirt to garbage.

A small tornado funnel sucks part of the cloud with it. It becomes the color of the cloud—maybe white or gray. Once the tornado touches down, it begins to pick up objects from the ground. For instance, if a tornado picks up dirt from a field containing a large amount of clay, the debris cloud can appear red in color.

Tornado Averages

A tornado travels with its parent thunderstorm. The amount of time the tornado lasts is **proportional** to its strength. Most tornadoes last for a few minutes, but a powerful one such as the Tri-State Tornado can last for several hours. An average tornado's rate of speed is about 30 miles per hour, and its path is only about 150 feet wide. Most travel only a few miles before dying out, though some can travel for many miles. Tornadoes are most likely to occur in the late afternoon to early evening, but they can happen anytime.

Tornadoes can also happen at any time of the year. In the southern states, they are most frequent in the spring. March, April, and May bring the most tornadoes to southern states. As the months pass, there are fewer and fewer tornadoes. By summer, the worst tornado season is over for these states.

In contrast, northern states such as Iowa, Illinois, and Indiana stay cold well into May. As warm air from the south travels north in the spring, these areas are still cold. For this reason, May, June, and July bring the most tornadoes in the Great Lakes region. The fewest tornadoes are formed during the winter, when the sun has little power to heat up winds from the south. Of course, the average tornado does not describe every tornado. In fact, some tornadoes never even touch the ground.

Other tornadoes strike outside of tornado season. When they do hit, they often catch people unprepared. For instance, in January 1999, a fierce storm system raced through western Tennessee. Multiple tornadoes struck, flipping mobile homes, cars, and trucks. Homes and businesses were ripped to pieces. Eight people died.

People who did survive often had only seconds to react. One woman had no idea a tornado was coming until her sister called to tell her. She and her family ran to a bathroom for shelter as the tornado winds took the roof off the house. Although her home was destroyed, she and her family lived. Even emergency workers barely had any warning about the storm. In one town, firefighters were told to leave their fire station just minutes before a tornado destroyed it. This tornado simply did not fit the average profile.

You can clearly see the path taken by this destructive out-of-season tornado.

Waterspouts: Watery Tornadoes

One kind of tornado has a very different life from the ones that form over land. A tornado that forms over an ocean or a lake is **classified** as a waterspout. It looks almost like a land tornado, with a big, dark parent cloud above and a twisting rope of wind hanging down toward the water.

A waterspout, however, does not have a debris cloud. The debris cloud of a tornado over land **corresponds** to a spray ring of a waterspout. A spray ring is a wet cloud of ocean or lake water that is kicked up at the base of the twisting rope of the waterspout. The waterspout lifts up the water in this ring.

Sometimes when a strong waterspout touches down, it can lift tons of water, along with fish, frogs, turtles, and other small creatures in the water. When the waterspout slows down, it drops all its water and the animals as well.

Can you imagine how surprised you would be to see fish and frogs raining out of the sky? Well, ancient people who saw this were very surprised indeed. Now we know that the water and objects picked up by a waterspout can travel long distances before being dropped to the ground or back in the water.

The biggest **proportion** of fish and frogs that are sucked up in waterspouts usually do not survive their trip into the heights of the atmosphere. A pair of frogs did make it back down to Earth alive once, however. The frogs were sealed inside a large hailstone that fell on Dubuque, Iowa, in 1882. When the ice melted, the frogs hopped away as if nothing had happened!

Waterspouts are harder to study than tornadoes because most people do not live on the ocean to notice them or to record what they see. Some sailors have been close to a waterspout and have recorded their experience by drawing pictures or taking photographs. Others have described how the wind and the funnel cloud behaved. Yet almost no one had studied waterspouts until the Lower Keys Waterspout Project in 1969. The project began as a result of the rainy spring and summer of 1968 in the Florida Keys. During this time, the islands in the Florida Keys got more rain than ever before in recorded history. The people of the Keys saw more than 100 waterspouts. Although many of these waterspouts stayed off shore and hurt no one, others were much more **aggressive**, lifting boats and damaging shorelines.

The huge number of waterspouts created such worry that some scientists were motivated to study waterspouts intensely. In 1969, they began the Lower Keys Waterspout Project. Scientists on the project worked with the National Hurricane Center and the National Oceanic and Atmospheric Administration (NOAA). By flying airplanes through storms to measure wind and air pressure, they were able to document and **classify** 95 waterspouts and uncover many of the conditions that create a waterspout.

The scientists learned that the first sign of a waterspout is a dark spot on the water, which comes from wind blowing down and swirling the water around. The wind draws in air and grows in size and strength. The strong, swirling wind creates a spray ring at the spot where the funnel touches the water. Next, water is pulled up the walls of the funnel. Then, the funnel moves across the water. The waterspout ends when the funnel runs into cold air. At that point, the funnel lifts off the water and falls apart.

Like tornadoes, waterspouts do not last long. Most last fewer than 30 minutes, and small waterspouts last only about 8 minutes. However, the damage they can do can be extreme, especially in **proportion** to the amount of time the waterspouts last. Waterspouts that form close to land can be especially **risky**. In one case, the ropes holding a 5-ton houseboat to its anchors were ripped off. Then, the boat was lifted about 10 feet off the water and carried to shore. The waterspout dropped the boat on top of an 8-foot-tall wooden post that was 100 feet away from where the boat had been floating. Luckily, the boat's owners were not on board.

In another case, a strong waterspout lifted a crowded motorboat out of the water in Venice, Italy. With passengers on board, the boat weighed 25 tons. Within 30 seconds, the waterspout lifted the boat, turned it around, and then dropped it back into the water. In this case, all 18 passengers were killed.

A waterspout

One Captain's Account

One experienced boat captain in the Florida Keys tells this story about a time that she was caught close to a waterspout.

"One time, another captain and I were on our big cruising sailboat far out in the ocean. It was night, and we had our anchor down. The night had been stormy and it was very humid. We woke up and heard a low whine. 'What is this?' we thought. We came out on the deck of the boat. We could see all around us because the sky was lit up with flashes of heat lightning. Then we saw that about 300 yards from us was a huge waterspout. It was dropping down from low clouds. As we watched, it bent hard to the right about 15 feet. Then, it hit the water and began moving toward us. It was terrifying. We wondered if we should put the sails up and sail away, but we knew we could never get away fast enough.

"I've often seen waterspouts from far away, but this was different. We didn't know what the waterspout would do. We kept watching, and lucky for us it twisted away from us and then fell apart into nothing. It had lasted for only a few moments. We were so lucky that it did not hit our boat, but it certainly could have caused severe damage."

This captain was indeed lucky that the waterspout fell apart before it reached her boat. Others are not so lucky. Her experience has taught her to respect the great power of the wind. Even though she sees waterspouts all the time, she knows that only the most foolish boaters would ever get close to one.

CHAPTER 5

How Did the Forecasters Do?

Remember how the worst tornadoes on the Fujita scale are **classified**? They are F5 tornadoes. The stories of the worst F5 tornadoes of the twentieth century show how far we have come in our ability to predict tornadoes and prevent loss of life and property.

The Tri-State Tornado of 1925

You've already read about some of the damage caused by the Tri-State Tornado of March 18, 1925. It was different from most tornadoes. Tragically, it killed more people than any other tornado. It destroyed more towns. It also moved faster and stayed on the ground longer than any other tornado in recorded history.

The Tri-State Tornado began with cold air from Canada that moved south over the northern plains. It headed straight for a mass of warm, moist air from the Gulf of Mexico.

Where were the weather forecasters? In 1925, the U.S. Weather Bureau (now called the National Weather Service) had been around for 55 years. However, the agency had primitive instruments and didn't know much about tornadoes. The bureau had a complete **inability** to predict the **risk** posed by the storm.

After landing in Missouri, the Tri-State Tornado traveled in a straight path over rivers, mountains, and plains. None of these natural features could stop the tornado. As the storm moved east through Missouri, conditions showed no signs of **improving**.

The tornado raged through farms and towns, killing 11 people. The storm traveled so close to the ground that the funnel cloud could not be seen. It looked like a fast-moving black fog.

The storm did its greatest damage in Illinois. As it struck the state, the sky grew dark. One newspaper reported this account of the weather: "All morning, before the tornado, it had rained. The day was dark and gloomy. The air was heavy. There was no wind. Then, the drizzle increased. The heavens seemed to open, pouring down a flood. The day grew black....

"Then the air was filled with 10,000 things. Boards, poles, cans, garments, stoves, whole sides of the little frame houses, in some cases the houses themselves, were picked up and smashed to Earth. And living beings, too. A baby was blown from its mother's arms. A cow, picked up by the wind, was hurled into the village restaurant."

The same newspaper wrote about a young schoolgirl. She had been in school when the tornado struck her town. The girl had no idea that bad weather was on the way. At that time, schools were not equipped with tornado sirens, and no warning had come from the demolished towns nearby.

The girl described how her classroom suddenly became so dark that the students couldn't see. She said, "All the children rushed to the windows. Teacher was mad. She made us go back to our seats again. All we could see at the windows was that it was black—like night almost.

"Then, the wind struck the school. The walls seemed to fall in, all around us. Then, the floor at one end of the building gave way. We all slipped or slid in that direction. If it hadn't been for the seats it would have been like sliding down a cellar door. I can't tell you what happened then. I can't describe it. I can't bear to think about it.

Children all about me were cut and bleeding. They cried and screamed. It was something awful. I had to close my eyes."

Hardest hit was Murphysboro, Illinois, where 234 people were killed. One schoolgirl remembered how a dark cloud cut short her afternoon recess. She said, "The windows began to break and my teacher sent us into the hallway. Afterwards, when it had stopped raining, we were dismissed from school. The teachers warned us to watch for downed electrical wires.

"On the way home I climbed over an uprooted tree and saw a shoe with a foot in it. As I approached my house, I noticed the roof from the house across the alley leaning against a tree in my backyard. The four sides of the house were laid flat like a house of cards." Incredibly, this girl's house was still standing, although the roof had been blown off.

The people of Illinois were completely surprised by the storm. It had wiped out communications from the demolished towns it had passed through. The **inability** to communicate meant that it took some time before neighboring towns noticed the destruction and sent help for the bleeding and shaken survivors.

A funeral was in progress in this Murphysboro, Illinois church when the Tri-State Tornado hit.

More than 600 people died from the tornado in Illinois. Survivors worked to free others from the wreckage. Injured people were taken to the few buildings that still stood after the storm. These buildings were made into temporary hospitals.

As the tornado passed out of Illinois and into Indiana, it crossed the Wabash River. There, it picked up mud and water, filling the air with wet dirt. The tornado then dumped dirt and debris on the other side of the river, leaving the **inevitable** smashed buildings and covering everything and everyone with a thick coat of black mud. At this point, the tornado picked up speed. It began traveling across country at a very **aggressive** rate, more than 70 miles per hour.

Finally, after 219 miles of destruction, the Tri-State Tornado ran into a mass of cold air that stopped its winds and ended its life. The tornado had killed 689 people and injured almost 2,000. It had caused millions of dollars in damage.

Could the Tri-State Tornado Happen Today?

A tornado the size of the Tri-State Tornado could hit the United States again. However, today the National Weather Service has the most sophisticated weather warning system in the world. People can hear forecasts for tornadoes and severe weather well in advance, and can make plans to keep safe. In addition, TV and radio stations now send weather warnings out regularly. With so much modern science at work predicting tornadoes, it is unlikely that a tornado today could kill as many people as the Tri-State Tornado of 1925.

The Outbreak of 1965

The Tri-State Tornado seems to have been one large tornado. Its path of destruction was continuous. There were very few **sites** where the tornado seemed to have weakened. In contrast, the tornado event of 1965 was an outbreak. On the evening of Sunday, April 11, 1965, a huge storm system over the Great Lakes region gave birth to almost 50 tornadoes. Two of the tornadoes were ranked at F5. With a death toll of 256 people, the Outbreak of 1965 is considered the second most damaging tornado event of the century. How did the U.S. Weather Bureau do in forecasting this event?

The bureau had been issuing tornado forecasts since 1952. By 1965, the bureau was using data from radar and from a satellite in orbit to predict the weather. In the days before the April 1965 outbreak, the U.S. Weather Bureau knew that bad weather was coming. Meteorologists had issued tornado warnings to all the states in the Great Lakes area.

However, many TV and radio stations did not relay the warnings. At that time, radio stations were not required to broadcast weather warnings. In fact, **irrational** as it sounds today, most radio station managers thought that the warning messages were only for cases of enemy attack. In 1965, towns did not use their sirens to alert their citizens of weather danger, either. Like the radio warnings, sirens were thought to exist only to warn of an enemy attack.

Also, communities in 1965 experienced power failures during bad storms, just as people do today. People who had seen the tornadoes pass by could not warn others that the tornadoes were coming because so many phone lines had been destroyed.

Twin funnels can be seen in this photo from the Outbreak of 1965.

Because of all the communication failures, hundreds of people died in the 1965 tornado outbreak, and many more lost homes. Businesses and farmlands were ruined. After the 1965 disaster, the U.S. Weather Bureau made important changes. It started an outdoor warning system of tornado sirens. It helped establish a radio network that would get weather warnings to people in every town. It decided that radio stations should be allowed to broadcast all night during a disaster, even if the stations were only licensed to broadcast until sunset.

Finally, the bureau began to make its warnings simpler so that all listeners would understand when tornadoes were in their area. Did you ever hear of a tornado watch or a tornado warning? Those terms started as a result of the April 1965 outbreak. A tornado *watch* means that tornadoes are possible in an area, although none have been spotted. A tornado *warning* means that meteorologists have spotted a tornado and are tracking its path.

The Super Outbreak of 1974

The tornado event in April 1974 is ranked as one of the worst tornado disasters of the century for several reasons. First, the huge storm over the Midwest and South gave birth to an incredible 148 tornadoes. Five of these were considered to be of F5 intensity, causing serious damage. Second, the combined distances of the 1974 tornadoes added up to 2,500 miles, far more than any previous outbreak.

However, there had been great **improvement** in tornado warning systems since the 1965 outbreak. By the 1970s, the National Weather Service, as the U.S. Weather Bureau was now named, had studied tornado weather closely. The prediction and **detection** of tornadoes were much more sophisticated. Also, tornado warning systems had been in place for some time.

In early April 1974, the **improvements** in the warning system became a matter of life and death. A total of 330 people were killed in the 1974 super outbreak. More people died than in the 1965 outbreak, but the loss of life could have been much greater. The path of destruction was much longer than the path of the Tri-State Tornado or of the 1965 outbreak.

The first days of April were stormy all over the Midwest. On April 1, two days before the major outbreak, weather forecasters issued severe weather watch notices for 11 areas. They were right to do so, because these storms would create 20 tornadoes.

Learning of the tornadoes, Midwesterners were **motivated** to listen to the weather closely and to watch the skies. By April 2, the storm clouds still showed the **risk** of more tornadoes. National forecasters sent a message to many radar stations to keep a close eye out for tornado activity. These warnings gave forecasters and local residents time to prepare for the worst.

Before dawn on April 3, there were severe weather watches posted for several areas. By midday, the National Weather Service tried to pinpoint the **approximate** area where the worst storms would hit. The service issued 150 tornado warnings. The huge outbreak of tornadoes came between 3:00 p.m. and 10:00 p.m. on April 3.

Of course, not everyone heard the weather warnings, nor could everyone get out of the path of the huge tornadoes. One F5 tornado struck Xenia, Ohio. Ruth Venuti was 18 years old at the time, and she was at Xenia High School. On the afternoon of April 3, she was looking out the school window, waiting for her ride home. Then she saw the huge funnel cloud bearing down on the building. She raced into the auditorium, where the drama club was practicing for a play. She burst in on the rehearsal and called for everyone to come and see. The drama teacher ran with the students to see the storm and then rushed everyone into the central hallway of the school. They lay flat on the floor, hoping they would be safe.

The tornado struck the school dead on. It threw mud, wood, glass, and huge chunks of the school building through the air. When the tornado passed after 4 minutes, the top floor of the school was gone. Part of the auditorium roof had caved in. Right on the stage where the students had been practicing just moments before was an upside-down school bus. Luckily for young Ruth and her school friends, none of the students were killed or seriously injured.

When a tornado strikes, even the best weather **detection** equipment and warning system can only tell you that it's time to get to a safe place. You also need to know how to plan for a tornado—and how to react when one hits.

CHAPTER 6

Tornado Safety

Surviving a tornado **represents** a combination of luck and planning. You are lucky if you're not directly in the tornado's path. The planning takes over when your luck runs out. You'll need a plan when you find yourself on or near the path of a tornado.

Plan Ahead

Some communities, especially those in Tornado Alley, have created disaster plans for an entire town. For example, many towns have warning sirens that blow in a particular pattern if a tornado is about to strike. Many towns also have evacuation routes in the case of severe weather, flood, or another disaster.

If you live anyplace that gets tornadoes, you should make a family plan for surviving a tornado. This plan is important to make before a tornado strikes because the time between a tornado warning and the actual tornado strike may be as short as 5 minutes. That's not much time for digging around in the junk drawer to look for flashlight batteries. To make your plan, talk to your family members and determine the safest place to go in your home if a tornado were to strike.

As part of your plan, learn where the shutoff valves are for water, gas, and electricity in your home. That way you can stop the house from flooding or stop a fire from starting. Once you have made your plan, practice it with your family. Think about the places where you spend the most time. Each place should **represent** part of your safety plan.

What to Do If You're at Home

If you hear a tornado watch, you should listen to a TV or radio station for weather updates. You should also watch the sky for tornadoes. Look for a funnel cloud and listen for a fast, howling wind.

If you hear a tornado warning, it means that a tornado or a thunderstorm with the conditions that produce tornadoes has been reported in your area. You're in danger, but disaster is not **inevitable**. You should go to a safe place in your home right away.

The safest place to be when a tornado strikes your home is underground or as low to the ground as possible. If you live in a house with a basement, the basement is probably the safest place to shelter from the storm. Choose a place away from windows, which could break and send flying glass all over a room. Also, you should figure out the **approximate** location of heavy objects on the floor above, such as the refrigerator or a piano. Choose a safe place that is not right underneath such objects. If the floor were weakened by high winds, you would not want these objects to come crashing down on top of you.

If you live in an apartment building or dormitory, go to the lowest floor of the building. Many large buildings have safe areas that are large enough to shelter everyone in the building. If there is no such place, look for an interior hallway with no windows. Also, use the stairs instead of the elevator to get to the lowest floor. You could get trapped in an elevator if the power failed.

If you live in a mobile home, you should be very **motivated** to make a tornado plan because even a small tornado can damage a mobile home. In severe weather, you should get out and go to a sturdy structure nearby. If there is no sturdy structure nearby, you are still safer outside than in a mobile home. Find a ditch or a low place in the ground to lie in. If you can't find a low place, lie flat on open ground away from trees and cars, which could be blown on top of you.

Storm Cellars and Safe Rooms

Many people in Tornado Alley and other parts of the country dig storm cellars. A storm cellar can be a deep hole in the side of a hill. It has a door that lies flat on the ground so that it cannot be ripped off by high wind.

Storm cellars are built of concrete and steel. The cellars are designed to withstand winds up to 250 miles per hour and debris flying at 100 miles per hour.

Sometimes a safe room is built into a new house and is used for a different purpose during calm weather. For example, a bathroom can be built as a safe room with concrete

A storm cellar was the only part of a Kansas family's home that was not damaged by a tornado in 2003.

walls, no windows, a steel door, and good ventilation. When a tornado is near, the whole family takes shelter in the room until the danger passes. Such a room is convenient because warning times for tornadoes can be so short. A family may not have time to get to an outdoor storm cellar before disaster strikes.

Once you have determined a safe place in your home, gather the supplies you'll need during a tornado. You should collect a first-aid kit, a battery-powered radio, flashlights, and extra batteries. You should also stock your safe place with canned food and water in case you are stuck in this place for a long time.

Don't Watch!

When you are reading Red Cross advice about tornado safety on a sunny, calm afternoon, it is easy to think sensibly and plan to find shelter well in advance of danger. However, even the most experienced weather observers have taken foolish **risks** in order to watch storms.

One reporter from Tornado Alley knew the terrible force of tornado winds. He had grown up with tornado danger and had even worked as a weather forecaster. On June 3, 1980, he was in his 11-story apartment building when he saw a huge storm approaching. From his window, he could see tornadoes dangling from black clouds. Instead of racing for the basement, the reporter went to the roof of his building with his camera. He shook with fear as the wind blew around him, realizing that the tornado could hop right over the city and land on top of his building. He was lucky to make it to safety.

Many people who know the dangers of severe weather are drawn outside to see the power of Mother Nature at her worst. In fact, there are people known as storm chasers who will travel hundreds of miles to observe tornadoes and other storms. Some like to photograph storms. Others just like to see how bad the weather can get. Storm chasing can be *extremely* dangerous. If you are ever in a dangerous storm, remember that tornadoes are unpredictable! The smartest place to be while a tornado is raging is far away from it.

What to Do If You're in a Car

If you are in a car or other vehicle, you are also in great danger. A car can easily become a deathtrap when high winds pick it up and hurl it through the air.

Remember, most tornadoes move at **approximately** 30 miles per hour. However, some tornadoes move faster than 30 miles per hour. Others have curving, unpredictable paths. In such cases, you are not safe inside a car. If you are in a car when a tornado strikes, you should park the car safely away from traffic, get out, and go to a sturdy building. If there is no sturdy building nearby, lie down with your hands over your head. If possible, lie in a ditch or low place on the ground.

Unfortunately, it is not always possible to follow this advice. One man in Nebraska was caught completely by surprise in a truck in June 2003. He stopped his truck when he drove into the high winds of a terrible tornado, but he did not have time to get out. Suddenly a huge hailstone the size of a baseball smashed into the windshield of his truck on the passenger side. He put his arms over his head to protect his face from flying glass. He was lucky to have survived the storm.

What should a driver do when a tornado approaches?

What to Do If You're at School

If you are at school when severe weather strikes, you should follow the instructions of your teacher. If you live in Tornado Alley or near it, chances are good that you've been through many tornado drills. You know what the tornado siren at your school sounds like. You also know how to walk quietly and calmly in a line to the safest place in the building and to wait there until your teachers say that it's safe to leave.

Schools are responsible for their students' safety, and principals and teachers prepare carefully for tornadoes. They make **adjustments** in their plan that **correspond** to the number of students in the school and the time of day the severe weather strikes. If severe weather is in the area at the end of the school day, students will not be sent home. They are in much greater danger in a bus or car than they are in a sturdy school building.

Large rooms such as the gymnasium, auditorium, or lunchroom are the worst places to be in a school building. Usually, these rooms cannot stand up to tornado-strength winds.

A tornado drill

What to Do If You're Asleep

What do you do if you are asleep when a tornado comes? You cannot possibly be listening to weather reports all night long. Some people solve this problem by buying a special radio called a NOAA Weather Radio. These radios solve our **inability** to listen to every announcement. They are designed to receive a special tone that comes with a weather warning. The tone turns the radio on. It makes a loud alarm sound and then the **corresponding** warning information follows. The radios can be programmed to set off an alarm for bulletins in certain areas. This type of radio is especially useful in hospitals, schools, and other gathering places.

Tornado Myths

There are many myths about things you "should" do if a tornado strikes. In fact, these myths are **risky** things that you should *not* do! They include the following:

- Do *not* try to take shelter from a tornado under a bridge or a highway overpass. High winds can send chunks of concrete falling down from every spot. You are also a target for high winds anytime you are above ground in a tornado.

- Do *not* open the windows of a house to equalize the air pressure. By the time the tornado hits, the windows will be broken and smashed anyway.

- Do *not* assume that you are safe just because you live in a big city. Although wind disturbance from tall buildings does occasionally redirect tornadoes, you should take tornado warnings very seriously no matter where you live.

You could get a powerful shock in an area where power lines are down.

After the Tornado Passes

After a tornado passes, listen to the radio for instructions and information. Stay away from any **site** where power lines have fallen. Even after power lines are knocked over by wind, they may still be carrying electricity. Be especially careful when a power line is wet or is hanging into a puddle. You could get a big shock from touching just the water.

Many tornadoes damage gas lines in homes and along the street. Gas could be filling the air inside and around your home. For this reason, you should not light a candle to help you see. The flame could ignite the gas from the broken gas line and start a huge fire.

Learning about tornadoes is the first part of tornado safety. The second part is planning. However, you don't have to do all the planning on your own. If you look around, you may notice that plans are already in place at your school, in large buildings, in apartment complexes, and even in your hometown. Knowledge and good planning will help you to safely get out of the way when wild winds start to blow.

Glossary

adjustments slight changes made to improve a situation or object

aggressive showing strength or violence

alternating switching back and forth between two or more things. An **alternative** is something that you can choose to do or have instead of something else.

approximately almost. **Approximate** means nearly correct.

classified put into a category

correspond to be in agreement with or to relate to something closely. **Corresponding** means having the same relationship to each of two different objects.

detect to find something that is difficult to locate. **Detection** is the process of finding something.

disputing arguing against something. A **dispute** means an argument.

extensive spread over a wide area; involving a great amount. Something that is done **extensively** is done a great deal.

improvement the process of making something greater or increasing the value of something

inability a lack of power to perform an action or task

induced caused some action or condition

inevitable unavoidable

intervened came between; also, got involved in order to change something. To **intervene** is to take action to change something or to stop it from happening.

justifiable able to be shown as fair or reasonable. To **justify** is to give a reason that shows why something is fair or reasonable.

motive a reason that moves someone to perform some action. **Motivated** means provided with a reason to do something.

originated began. To **originate** means to start or begin.

perilous involving danger or risk. A **peril** is a danger.

preferable more desirable. Something that is **preferred** is liked more than other things.

primarily mostly; for the most part

proportional corresponding in size or degree. **Proportion** means a fair or equal share or a percentage.

rational reasonable or logical. **Irrational** means not following logic or reason.

represents shows, or takes the place of something else

resume to begin again

risks dangers or possibilities of loss. **Risky** means dangerous.

significant having importance or meaning

sites exact locations

skeptical filled with doubt that something is true or will really occur. **Skepticism** is an attitude of doubt.

striving making a very great effort; trying very hard. To have **striven** means to have struggled and tried hard.

subsided became less active or quieter. To **subside** is to become less intense or less active.

vigorous done with great energy; strong

virtually nearly or almost

Index